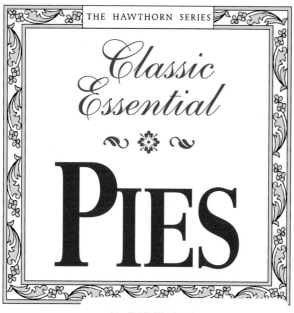

THE HAWTHORN SERIES

Classic
Essential

ॐ ❋ ॐ

PIES

CW00953834

Your Promise of Success

Welcome to the world of Confident Cooking, created for you in our test
kitchen, where recipes are double-tested by our team of home
economists to achieve a high standard of success.

M U R D O C H   B O O K S®

Sydney • London • Vancouver • New York

～ Pie Finishes ～

Decorating pies is an opportunity to use your imagination and creativity. Simple finishing touches can make all the difference to the appeal of a dish.

Here we show a few of the easy techniques that are used to decorate pies throughout the book. The step-by-step pictures with the recipes show other ways of finishing pies.

Edges

It is important to seal together the top and bottom layers of pastry on a double crust pie, so crimping of some sort is both necessary and decorative. The most common (and effective) way is to press the edges with the tines of a fork, or you could try pinching the edges together as shown.

Decorating the edge of single crust pies is not absolutely necessary, but adds a pretty touch.

Some pies made with puff pastry are baked on a flat baking tray, and the edges can be sealed by pressing firmly with a spoon or fork.

More traditional pies, such as Steak and Kidney, have a puff pastry top and no base. Strips of pastry are pressed on to the lip of the pie dish and brushed lightly with beaten egg, then the rolled out pastry is laid over the top. Press the pastry to seal, and then nick the edges with the blunt edge of a knife at 1 cm intervals to help the pastry to rise in flaky layers.

Decorations

With most pie recipes you will have a little

pastry left over after yo have trimmed the edge so use these to make decorations.

Traditionally, only savoury pies were decorated, so that swee and savoury pies could be told apart at a glanc Shapes such as flowers leaves or shells can be used where appropriate or fruit shapes to indicate the filling. Pil the trimmings together and re-roll them to abo 3 mm thick, and cut ou shapes. Leaves can be cut out freehand, but fo more complicated shapes use a small template made from cardboard. Biscuit cutters of various shap are ideal for cut-outs. make shells, use a roun scone cutter to make a

A spoon can be used to seal around the edges of puff pastry.

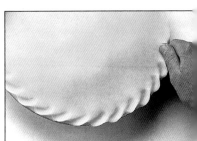

Pinch the edges of pastry together betwe thumb and forefinger to decorate and se

circle, then trim to a shell shape and score lines in the pastry. To attach to the pie, first glaze the top as directed in the recipe, then place your cut-outs in position and glaze them as well.

Lattice

Making a lattice top is quite simple with a little practice. Roll out the pastry to a circle on a sheet of baking paper, then use a small sharp knife or fluted pastry wheel to cut strips of pastry to the desired thickness (use a ruler to help if you like). On another sheet of baking paper, arrange half the strips vertically about 1 cm apart, keeping longer lengths in the centre and shorter ones on the outsides. Carefully fold back alternate strips, and lay a piece horizontally across the remaining strips. Fold the strips back over the pastry, then fold the underneath pieces back and place another horizontal piece over. Repeat with the remaining strips.

Refrigerate the pastry until firm, then invert onto the pie and remove the paper. Press the edges together and trim the overhanging pastry. Glaze and bake as directed.

Cut strips of pastry with a fluted pastry wheel or a sharp knife.

To form a lattice top for pies, interweave the strips of pastry.

If you want complicated shapes for decoration, use a template as a guide.

Trim circles of pastry to a shell shape and score lines on the top with a sharp knife.

Savoury Pies

~ Family Style Meat Pie ~

Preparation time:
30 minutes
Total cooking time:
2 hours

Serves 4–6

1 kg round steak	**2 tablespoons tomato**
¼ cup plain flour	**paste**
salt and freshly ground	**1 tablespoon**
black pepper	**Worcestershire**
2 tablespoons oil	**sauce**
1 medium onion,	**375 g frozen puff**
chopped	**pastry, thawed**
1 cup beef stock	**1 egg, lightly beaten,**
	for glazing

1 ~ Trim the excess fat and sinew from the meat and cut the meat into 2 cm cubes. Place the plain flour in a plastic bag. Add some salt and pepper and then shake the bag to mix well. Add the cubed meat to the bag and toss gently until well coated with the flour. Remove the meat from the bag and shake off any excess flour.
2 ~ Heat the oil in a hcavy-based pan. Add the meat to the pan, in batches, and cook quickly until browned. Drain on paper towels. Add the onions to the pan and cook for 5 minutes or until soft.

3 ~ Return the meat to the pan. Add the stock, tomato paste and Worcestershire sauce; bring to the boil. Reduce heat and simmer, covered, for 1½ hours, stirring occasionally. Remove the pan from heat and allow the meat to cool completely.
4 ~ Preheat the oven to 210°C (190°C gas). Transfer the meat mixture to a 4-cup capacity pie dish. Roll out the pastry until it is about 3 mm thick. Cut long strips of pastry to fit the lip of the dish. Press strips into place and seal any joins.

Place remaining pastry over the pie and press to seal onto pastry strip. Trim edges and decorate pie with leftover pastry. Brush with egg and bake for 30 minutes or until pastry is golden.
Note ~ A pie dish of any shape can be used. Check the cup capacity by standing the dish on a level surface and measuring water into it. Allow plenty of time for pastry to thaw before using it. Attempting to roll out the pastry before it is soft enough can lead to overworking of the dough and this can cause shrinkage.

Place the flour, salt and pepper in a plastic bag and shake the bag to mix well.

Press the pastry strips around the edge of the dish and press joins together to seal.

~ Ham and Chicken Pie ~

Preparation time:
40 minutes
Total cooking time:
1 hour
Serves 6–8

3 cups plain flour
180 g butter, chopped
1/3 cup iced water
1 egg, extra, lightly
   beaten, for glazing

Filling
1 kg chicken mince
1 teaspoon dried mixed
   herbs
2 eggs, lightly beaten

3 spring onions, finely
   chopped
2 tablespoons finely
   chopped fresh parsley
2 teaspoons French
   mustard
1/3 cup cream
salt and freshly ground
   pepper
200 g sliced leg ham

1. Preheat the oven to 180°C. Place flour and butter in a food processor. Process for 20 seconds or until mixture is fine and crumbly. Add almost all the water and process for 20 seconds or until the mixture comes together. Turn onto a lightly floured surface and press together until smooth. Roll out two-thirds of the pastry and line a 20 cm springform tin, leaving some pastry overhanging the sides. Cover with plastic wrap; refrigerate until required. Shape the remaining pastry into a flat disc, wrap in plastic and refrigerate.

2. **To make Filling:** Place the chicken, herbs, eggs, onions, parsley, mustard, cream, salt and pepper in a large bowl and stir with a wooden spoon until well combined. Divide the chicken mixture into three.
3. Place one portion into the pastry-lined tin and smooth the surface. Top with half the ham and then another chicken layer followed by the remaining ham and finally, chicken.

4. Brush around the inside edge of pastry with egg. Roll out remaining pastry and lay over top of the mixture. Press edges of the pastry together. Trim pastry edges with a sharp knife. Use your index finger to make indentations around edge. Decorate the top with pastry scraps. Brush top of the pie with beaten egg and bake for 1 hour or until golden brown. Serve the pie warm or at room temperature.

Process the flour and butter in a food processor until mixture comes together.

Combine the chicken, herbs, eggs, onions, parsley, mustard, cream, salt and pepper.

ayer the chicken mixture and the ham in
he pastry-lined tin, finishing with chicken.

Use a sharp knife to trim away the excess
pastry from the edges of the pie.

～ Shepherd's Pie ～

Preparation time:
30 minutes
Total cooking time:
1 hour

Serves 6

750 g lean cooked roast lamb	salt and pepper
25 g butter	*Potato Topping*
2 medium brown onions, finely chopped	1/2 cup hot milk
1/4 cup plain flour	30 g butter
1/2 teaspoon dry mustard	salt and freshly ground black pepper
1 1/2 cups chicken stock	4 large potatoes, cooked and mashed
2 tablespoons Worcestershire sauce	

1 ～ Brush an 8-cup capacity casserole with melted butter or oil. Preheat the oven to 210°C (190°C gas). Trim meat of excess fat and mince the meat or cut it into small cubes. Melt the butter in a large pan. Add the onions and cook until golden.

2 ～ Sprinkle the flour and mustard into pan and stir for 1 minute. Gradually add the stock and stir constantly until smooth. Bring the gravy to the boil and then reduce heat and simmer for 3 minutes.

3 ～ Add the meat and sauce to the pan and stir.

Season, to taste. Remove from heat and spoon into the casserole dish.

4 ～ **To make Potato Topping:** Add the milk, butter, and salt and pepper, to taste, to the mashed potato. Mix until smooth and creamy. Spread the mixture evenly over the meat and rough up the surface with a fork. Bake for 40–45 minutes or until the meat mixture is heated through and the potato topping is lightly golden.

Note ～ To make the topping for this dish especially creamy, mash the potato thoroughly and then push it through a sieve with the back of a spoon, before mixing in the milk and butter. Season with salt and pepper, to taste.

Gradually add the stock to the pan and use a wooden spoon to stir until smooth.

For very creamy topping, push the potato through a sieve with back of wooden spoon.

~ Steak and Kidney Pie ~

Preparation time:
20 minutes
Total cooking time:
1 hour 50 minutes

Serves 6

750 g round steak
4 lamb kidneys
2 tablespoons plain
flour
1 tablespoon oil
1 medium onion,
chopped
30 g butter
1 tablespoon
Worcestershire sauce
1 tablespoon tomato
paste
1/2 cup red wine

1 cup beef stock
125 g button
mushrooms, sliced
1/2 teaspoon dried
thyme
1/3 cup chopped fresh
parsley
salt and pepper
375 g packet frozen
puff pastry
1 egg, lightly beaten,
for glazing

1~Trim the meat of excess fat and sinew and cut into 2 cm cubes. Peel skin from the kidneys. Quarter the kidneys and trim away any fat or sinew. Place the flour in a plastic bag. Add the meat and kidneys to the bag and toss gently until well coated. Shake off excess flour. Heat the oil in a medium heavy-based pan. Add the onion and cook for 5 minutes or until soft. Remove from pan with a slotted spoon. Add the butter to pan. Brown the meat and kidneys in batches and then return it all to the pan.

2~Add Worcestershire sauce, tomato paste, red wine, beef stock, sliced mushrooms, thyme and parsley to the pan. Bring to the boil, reduce heat and simmer, covered, for 1 hour or until the meat is tender. Season with salt and pepper, to taste, and allow to cool. Spoon the meat mixture into a 6-cup capacity pie dish.
3~Preheat the oven to 210°C (190°C gas). Roll the puff pastry out on a

lightly floured surface s● that it is 4 cm larger tha● the dish. Cut thin strips from the pastry and press onto rim, sealing the joins. Place the pastry on top of the pie. Trim the edges and cut 2 slits in the pastry to allow steam to escape. Decorate the pie with leftover pastry and brus● the top with egg. Bake the pie for 35–40 minutes or until the pastry is golden brown.

In batches, cook meat and kidneys over high heat until browned. Drain on paper towels.

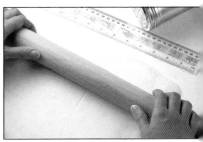

Roll the puff pastry out on a lightly floure● surface until it is 4 cm larger than the dis●

～Lamb and Filo Pie ～

Preparation time:
20 minutes
Total cooking time:
50 minutes

Serves 6

2 tablespoons oil
2 medium onions, chopped
1 teaspoon ground cumin
1 teaspoon ground coriander
1/2 teaspoon ground cinnamon

1 kg lamb mince
1/4 cup chopped fresh parsley
2 tablespoons chopped fresh mint
10 sheets filo pastry
250 g unsalted butter, melted

1～Heat the oil in a heavy-based pan. Add the onions and cook for 3 minutes or until just soft. Add the ground cumin, coriander and cinnamon, and cook, stirring constantly, for another minute.

2～Add the mince to the pan and cook over medium-high heat for 10 minutes or until the meat is brown and all the liquid has evaporated. Use a fork to break up any lumps of mince as it cooks. Add herbs and mix well. Set aside to cool.

3～Preheat the oven to 180°C. Lightly grease a

33 x 23 cm ovenproof dish with butter or oil. Remove 2 sheets of filo. Cover remainder with a clean, damp tea towel to prevent them drying out. Brush the top sheet of the removed pastry with melted butter. Place another 2 sheets of filo on top and brush the top one with butter. Line the baking dish with these 4 sheets, leaving the excess overhanging the dish.

4～Spread the lamb mixture over the pastry sheets and fold the overhanging pastry

over the filling. Butter 2 sheets of filo, place one on top of the other and fold in half. Place over the top of the filling and tuck in the edges. Butter the remaining 4 sheets and cut roughly into squares and then scrunch these over the top of the pie. Bake for 40 minutes or until pastry is crisp and golden.

As the mince cooks, press down on any lumps, using a fork to break them up.

Gently brush each top sheet of filo pastry with melted butter.

Spread lamb over the pastry and then fold the overhanging pastry over the filling.

Scrunch the squares of pastry roughly and place them over the top of the pie.

~ Bacon and Egg Pie ~

Preparation time:
**20 minutes +
refrigeration time**
Total cooking time:
50–55 minutes

Serves 4–6

1 sheet frozen
   shortcrust pastry,
   thawed
2 teaspoons oil
4 rashers bacon,
   chopped
5 eggs, lightly
   beaten

¹/₄ cup cream
1 sheet frozen puff
   pastry, thawed
1 egg, extra,
   lightly beaten, for
   glazing

1 ~ Preheat the oven to 210°C (190°C gas). Brush a 20 cm diameter loose-bottomed flan tin with melted butter or oil. Place the shortcrust pastry in prepared tin and trim the pastry edges. Cut a sheet of greaseproof paper to cover the pastry-lined tin. Spread a layer of dried beans or rice over the paper. Bake for 10 minutes and then discard paper and rice. Bake for another 5–10 minutes or until golden. Allow to cool.
2 ~ Heat the oil in a frying pan. Add the bacon and cook over medium heat for a few minutes or until lightly browned. Drain on paper towels and allow to cool slightly. Arrange the bacon over the pastry base and pour combined eggs and cream over the top. Brush the edges of pastry with extra egg, cover with puff pastry and press on firmly to seal. Trim pastry edges and decorate top with pastry scraps. Brush with extra egg and bake for 30–35 minutes or until puffed and golden. Serve warm or at room temperature.

Note ~ Blind baking the bottom pastry ensures a crisp crust. Bacon and Egg Pie is excellent for taking on picnics. It can be made a day ahead and refrigerated overnight. Leave it in the tin to transport to the picnic, then leave it on the base to make cutting easy. All you need to have with it is a simple salad.

Spread a layer of dried beans or rice over the paper before baking.

Carefully pour the combined eggs and cream over the top of the bacon.

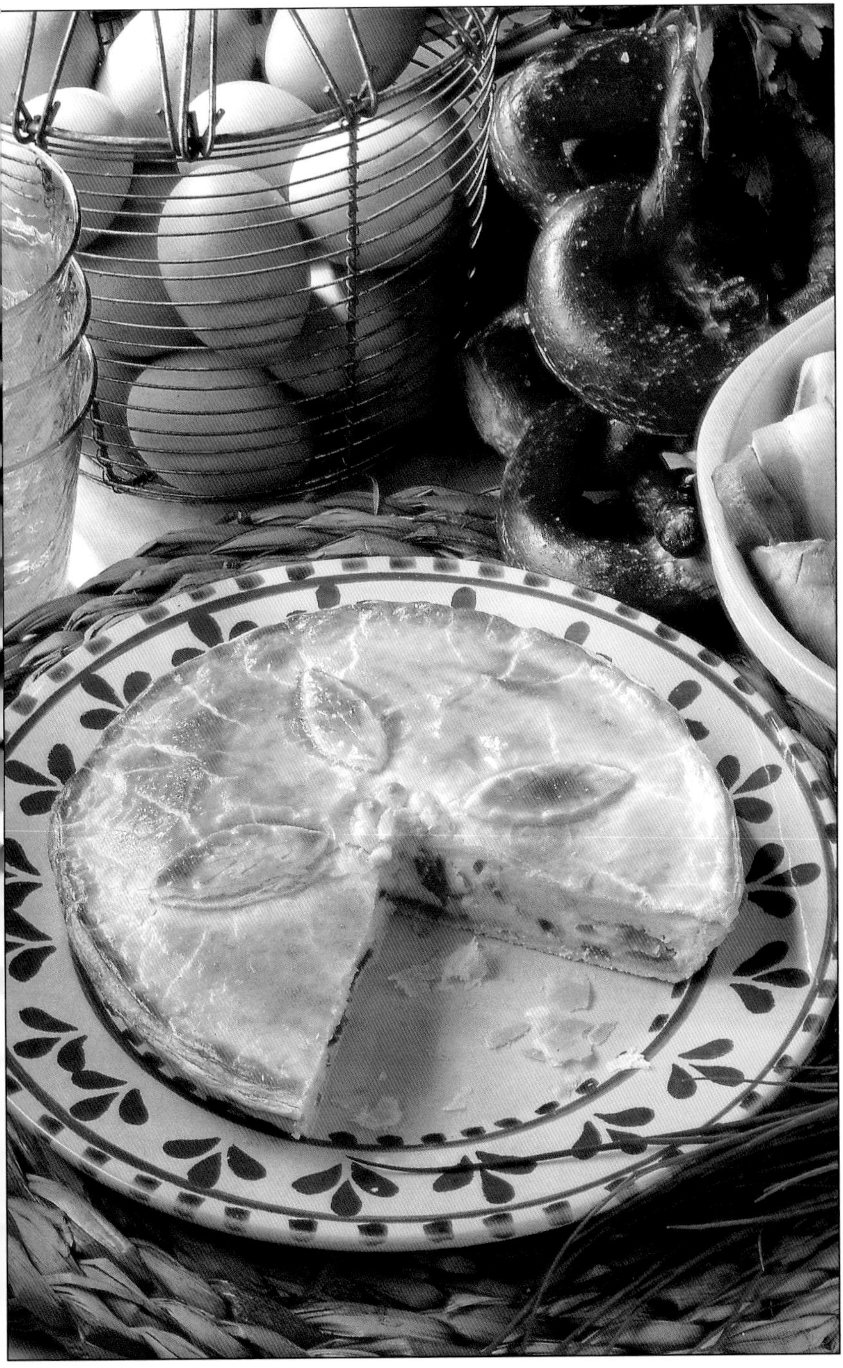

~ Irish Fish Pie ~

Preparation time:
40 minutes
Total cooking time:
45 minutes

Serves 4–6

750 g firm white fish fillets	**1 medium leek, extra, finely sliced**
1 large leek, chopped	**2 tablespoons plain flour**
2 strips lemon rind	**2 tablespoons finely chopped parsley**
1/4 teaspoon ground nutmeg	**1 kg potatoes, peeled and chopped**
8 peppercorns	**40 g butter**
2 bay leaves	**2 tablespoons cream**
6 stalks parsley	**salt and pepper**
2 1/2 cups milk plus some extra milk	
30 g butter	

1. Place fish fillets, leek, lemon rind, nutmeg, peppercorns, bay leaves and parsley in a pan. Add 2^{1}/2 cups milk and heat until simmering. Simmer, uncovered, over low heat for 15 minutes, or until the fish is cooked—cooking time depends on the thickness of the fillets. Carefully remove the fish fillets from pan. Strain the liquid and reserve for sauce.

2. Melt butter in a pan and add the extra leek. Cook over low heat for 10 minutes or until the leeks are very soft. Sprinkle flour over the remaining mixture in pan. Stir for 1 minute. Measure reserved fish poaching milk and add extra milk or cream, if necessary, to measure 1^{1}/2 cups altogether. Add gradually to the pan and stir until the mixture comes to the boil and thickens. Cook for another minute.

3. Cut the fish into chunky pieces and fold gently through the sauce with the parsley. Cook the potatoes in a large pan of boiling water until soft. Drain and mash with butter and cream. Season both the fish and potato mixture with salt and pepper, to taste.

4. Preheat the oven to 210°C (190°C gas). Grease a 6-cup capacity casserole dish and pour in the fish mixture. Top with mashed potatoes and use a fork to rough up the surface. Bake for 20 minutes or until the potato topping is golden.

When the fish is cooked, carefully remove it from the pan using a slotted spatula.

Place the mashed potatoes on top and rough up the surface with a fork.

～ Salmon Pie ～

Preparation time:
**25 minutes +
refrigeration**
Total cooking time:
40 minutes

Serves 4–6

60 g butter
**1 medium onion, finely
chopped**
**200 g button
mushrooms, sliced**
**2 tablespoons lemon
juice**
**220 g Atlantic salmon
fillet, boned, skinned,
cut into 2 cm pieces**
**2 hard-boiled eggs,
chopped**

**2 tablespoons fresh dill,
chopped**
**2 tablespoons parsley,
chopped**
**salt and freshly ground
black pepper**
1 cup cooked rice
1/4 cup cream
**375 g packet frozen
puff pastry**
**1 egg, lightly beaten,
for glazing**

1 ～ Brush an oven tray with melted butter or oil. Melt half the butter in a frying pan. Add the onion and cook for 5 minutes or until soft but not browned. Add the mushrooms and cook for another 5 minutes. Add the lemon juice to pan and stir to combine. Transfer the mixture to a bowl.

2 ～ Melt remaining butter in pan, add the salmon and cook for 2 minutes. Remove from heat, cool slightly and add the egg, dill, parsley and salt and pepper, to taste. Combine gently and set aside. Combine the rice and cream in a small bowl.

3 ～ Roll out half the pastry to a rectangle measuring 18 x 30 cm and place on the prepared tray. Spread half the rice mixture onto the pastry, leaving a 3 cm border all the way around. Top with the salmon mixture, then the mushroom mixture, and finish with the remaining rice.

4 ～ Roll out remaining pastry to 20 x 32 cm; place over the filling. Seal edges together, crimp to seal. Decorate with pastry cut-outs if you like. Refrigerate 30 minutes. Preheat oven to 210°C (190°C gas). Brush pie with beaten egg; bake 15 minutes. Reduce the heat to 180°C, bake for 15–20 minutes until golden.
Note ～ A 220 g can of red salmon can be used instead of fresh salmon.

*Add the sliced mushrooms to the softened
onions and stir for about 5 minutes.*

*When salmon has cooled slightly, add the
egg, dill, parsley, salt and pepper to pan.*

Spread the salmon mixture evenly over the rice layer.

Hang the remaining pastry over a rolling pin to make it easy to place over the filling.

～ Chicken Pot Pies ～

Preparation time:
20 minutes
Total cooking time:
30 minutes

Serves 4

2 teaspoons oil
1 small onion, finely chopped
1 small red capsicum, chopped
100 g pumpkin, peeled and cut into small cubes
1 medium carrot, peeled and cut into small cubes
1/2 cup frozen peas
130 g can corn kernels, drained
2 cups chopped cooked chicken
40 g butter
2 tablespoons plain flour
3/4 cup milk
3/4 cup chicken stock
salt and freshly ground black pepper
1 sheet frozen puff pastry, thawed
1 egg, lightly beaten, for glazing

1.～Brush four 1-cup capacity ramekins with melted butter. Preheat the oven to 210°C (190°C gas). Heat the oil in a small pan. Add the onions and capsicum and cook until just soft. Steam or microwave the pumpkin and carrot until tender. Drain the vegetables and combine in a bowl with the onion mixture, peas, corn and chicken; mix well. Melt the butter in a small pan. Add the flour and stir for 1 minute or until lightly golden and bubbling. Add the combined milk and stock gradually, stirring constantly until mixture boils and thickens. Season with salt and pepper, to taste.

2.～Remove from the heat, add to the chicken and vegetables and stir to combine. Spoon the mixture into the prepared ramekins.

3.～Cut four circles of pastry, slightly larger than the tops of the dishes. Score a pattern into the pastry, using a sharp knife.

4.～Place a circle over the filling of one dish and press the edges around the rim to seal. Repeat with remaining pastry and dishes. Cut small circles from the leftover pastry and place them on top of the pies, to decorate. Brush all over pastry with beaten egg. Bake the pies for 25 minutes or until the pastry is golden brown. Serve immediately.

Gradually add the combined milk and stock to mixture and stir until thick.

Add the white sauce to the chicken and vegetables and stir well.

Use the point of a sharp knife to score a pattern on the pastry circles.

Place a circle over the filling and press gently around the edges to seal.

～ Spinach Pie ～

Preparation time:
25 minutes
Total cooking time:
40 minutes

Serves 6–8

2 bunches English spinach	**5 eggs, lightly beaten**
1 tablespoon oil	**salt and freshly ground**
6 spring onions, finely chopped	**black pepper**
125 g feta cheese, crumbled	**16 sheets filo pastry**
3/4 cup grated Cheddar cheese	**1/3 cup olive oil**
	1 egg, extra, lightly beaten, for glazing
	1 tablespoon poppy seeds

1～Preheat the oven to 210°C (190°C gas). Brush a 30 x 25 cm baking dish with oil. Wash the spinach thoroughly and shred finely. Place in a large pan with water clinging to leaves and cook, covered, over low heat for 2 minutes or until just wilted. Cool, then wring any excess water from the spinach and spread out the strands.
2～Heat the oil in a small pan and cook the spring onions for 3 minutes or until soft. Transfer to a large bowl and add the spinach, cheeses, eggs, and salt and pepper, to taste. Stir until the cheeses are distributed evenly.
3～Place 1 sheet of pastry into the prepared dish, letting the edges hang over. Cover the remaining pastry with a clean, damp tea towel to prevent the pastry drying out. Brush the pastry in the dish with oil. Repeat the process with another 7 layers of pastry, brushing each sheet lightly with oil.
4～Spread the filling over the pastry, fold in the edges of pastry. Brush each remaining sheet of pastry lightly with oil and place on top of the pie. Tuck the edges of pastry down the sides, brush the top with the extra egg and sprinkle with poppy seeds. Bake for 35–40 minutes or until the pastry is golden. Serve immediately.
Note～Sesame seeds can be used instead of poppy seeds if you like.

After wringing excess water from the spinach, spread the strands out.

Stir the spinach and cheese mixture until cheeses are evenly distributed.

Gently brush each sheet of filo pastry lightly with olive oil.

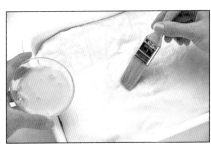

Carefully brush the top of the pie with the extra egg.

～ Vegetable Pie ～

Preparation time:
**40 minutes +
refrigeration**
Total cooking time:
1 hour

Serves 6

175 g butter
2 cups plain flour
1/4 cup iced water
1 tablespoon oil
1 medium onion, finely
  chopped
1 small red capsicum,
  chopped
1 small green capsicum,
  chopped
150 g pumpkin,
  chopped
1 small potato, chopped

100 g broccoli, cut into
  small florets
1 medium carrot,
  chopped
1/4 cup plain flour
1 cup milk
2 egg yolks
1/2 cup grated Cheddar
  cheese
1 egg, lightly beaten,
  for glazing

1 ～ Chop 125 g of the butter. Sift flour into a large bowl and add the chopped butter. Using your fingertips, rub the butter into the flour until the mixture is fine and crumbly. Add almost all the water and use a knife to mix to a firm dough, adding more water if necessary. Turn onto a lightly floured surface and press together until smooth. Divide the dough in half, roll out one portion and line a deep 21 cm fluted flan tin. Refrigerate for 20 minutes. Roll the remaining pastry out to a 25 cm diameter circle. Cut into strips and lay half of them on a sheet of baking paper, leaving a 2 cm gap between each strip. Interweave the remaining strips to form a lattice pattern. Cover with plastic wrap and refrigerate, keeping flat, until firm.
2 ～ Preheat the oven to 180°C. Cut a sheet of greaseproof paper to cover pastry-lined tin. Spread a layer of dried beans or rice over the paper. Bake 10 minutes, remove from oven and discard paper and beans, bake pastry for another 10 minutes or until golden. Remove; allow to cool.
3 ～ Heat the oil in a frying pan. Add the onion and cook for 2 minutes or until soft. Add the caspicums and cook, stirring, for another 3 minutes. Steam or boil the remaining vegetables until just tender; drain and cool. Combine the onions, capsicums and the other vegetables in a large bowl.
4 ～ Heat the remaining butter in a small pan. Add the flour and cook, stirring, for 2 minutes. Add the milk gradually, stirring until smooth between each addition. Stir constantly over medium heat until mixture boils and thickens. Boil for 1 minute and then remove from heat. Add the egg yolks and cheese; stir until smooth. Pour the sauce over the vegetables and stir to combine. Pour mixture into the pastry case and brush the edges with egg. Using the baking paper to help, invert the lattice over the vegetables, trim the edges and brush with a little beaten egg. Press edges lightly to seal to the cooked pastry. Brush the top with egg and bake for 30 minutes or until pastry is golden.

Add almost all the water to the bowl, mixing with a knife until a firm dough is formed.

Invert the lattice over the pie and slowly pull away the baking paper.

～Potato Pies ～

Preparation time:
25 minutes
Total cooking time:
55 minutes

Makes 8 pies

1 tablespoon oil
1 medium onion, finely chopped
1 clove garlic, crushed
500 g beef mince
2 tablespoons flour
2 cups beef stock
2 tablespoons tomato paste
1 tablespoon Worcestershire sauce
salt and pepper
4 sheets frozen shortcrust pastry, thawed
45 g butter
1/4 cup milk
5 large potatoes, cooked and mashed

1～Preheat the oven to 210°C (190°C gas). Heat oil in a pan, add onion and cook for 5 minutes, until soft. Add the garlic and cook for another minute. Add the mince and cook over medium heat for 5 minutes or until browned, breaking up any lumps with a fork.
2～Sprinkle the flour over the meat and stir to combine. Add the stock, paste, sauce, salt and pepper to pan; stir for 2 minutes. Bring to the boil and reduce heat slightly. Simmer, uncovered, for 5 minutes or until the mixture has reduced and thickened. Allow mixture to cool completely.
3～Brush eight 11 cm pie tins with melted butter or oil. Using a plate as a guide, cut the pastry into 14 cm circles, and line the pie tins. Cut sheets of greaseproof paper to cover each tin, spread dried beans or rice over the paper. Bake for approximately 7 minutes. Discard the paper and beans and cook the pastry for another 7 minutes. Allow to cool.
4～Spoon the filling into the pastry cases. Stir the butter and milk into the mashed potato and pipe over the top of the meat mixture. Bake for 20 minutes or until lightly golden. Serve immediately with vegetables of your choice. Steamed snow peas, broccoli, baby carrots, or grilled mushrooms and tomatoes are all suitable.
Note～Potato can be spread over filling, if you prefer. Rough up the surface with a fork.

Using a plate or a bowl as a guide, cut the pastry into 14 cm circles.

Pipe or spread the mashed potato over the top of the meat mixture.

～ Chicken and Leek Pie ～

Preparation time:
30 minutes
Total cooking time:
55 minutes

Serves 4–6

30 g butter
2 small leeks, white
part only, thinly sliced
3 rashers bacon,
chopped
3 chicken breast fillets,
cut into thin strips

½ cup cream
2 egg yolks
salt and pepper
2 sheets frozen puff
pastry, thawed
1 egg, lightly beaten,
for glazing

1～Brush a flat oven tray lightly with melted butter or oil. Melt the butter in a frying pan and cook the leeks over medium-low heat for about 10 minutes until very soft and lightly golden, stirring occasionally. Transfer to a plate and set aside.
2～Add the bacon to the pan and cook until lightly browned, remove and set aside. Add the chicken to pan and cook for about 5 minutes, until lightly browned. Remove from pan and drain on paper towels.
3～Wipe out the pan with paper towels.

Return the leeks, bacon and chicken to the pan. Add the combined cream and yolks, stir over low heat for 2 minutes and then season with salt and pepper, to taste. Transfer to a bowl to cool.
4～Preheat the oven to 210°C (190°C gas). Cut thin strips from around the edge of one of the pastry sheets and set the strips aside. Place this sheet on the prepared tray. Spread the chicken and leek mixture onto the pastry, leaving a 2 cm border all around. Top with the second sheet of pastry and

crimp the edges together to seal. Decorate with the cut strips of pastry— the strips can be twisted to give the effect shown in the picture. Prick the pastry with a fork to allow steam to escape, and brush the pastry with beaten egg. Bake for 30 minutes or until the top is puffed and golden brown.

Cook the leeks over a medium-low heat until soft and lightly golden.

Cook the chicken until lightly browned, remove from pan, drain on paper towels.

Add the combined cream and egg yolks to the pan and stir with a wooden spoon.

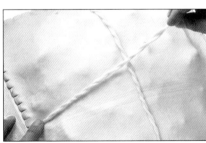

The strips of pastry can be twisted to make an attractive decoration.

~ Rabbit Pie ~

Preparation time:
**45 minutes +
refrigeration and
overnight soaking**
Total cooking time:
2 hours 45 minutes

Serves 4

1 tablespoon vinegar
1/2 teaspoon salt
1 rabbit, about 1.25 kg,
  cut into 12 portions
1/4 cup plain flour
salt and pepper
1/4 cup olive oil plus
  1 tablespoon, extra
2 rashers bacon,
  roughly chopped
2 medium onions, finely
  chopped

1 green cooking apple,
  peeled, cored and
  chopped
12 pitted prunes
1 tablespoon plain flour
1 tablespoon soft brown
  sugar
1 teaspoon dried thyme
375 ml beer or cider
375 g packet puff pastry
1 egg yolk mixed with
  1 teaspoon water, for
  glazing

1 ~ Add the vinegar and salt to a large bowl of water. Add rabbit portions and leave to soak overnight in the refrigerator. Drain and rinse well. Dry with paper towels. Combine the flour, salt and pepper in a large bowl, toss rabbit in seasoned flour.

2 ~ Preheat the oven to 180°C. Heat 1/4 cup of olive oil in a large heavy-based frying pan. Cook the rabbit quickly, in batches, over medium heat until browned. Transfer to a 2-litre casserole dish.

3 ~ Heat the extra oil in frying pan; add bacon, onions, apple and prunes. Cook over medium heat for 5 minutes or until lightly browned. Sprinkle the flour and brown sugar over the mixture and stir to combine. Cook, stirring, for 5 minutes. Pour on the beer or cider and stir constantly for 3 minutes or until thickened. Stir in the thyme. Pour the mixture over the rabbit. Cover the dish with a tight-fitting lid. Bake for 2 hours or until tender.

4 ~ Transfer the mixture to a deep 1.25-litre pie dish with a rim. Cool the mixture and then refrigerate until it is cold. When cold, place a pie funnel in the centre of the dish. Roll the pastry out so that it is about 5 cm larger than the top of the pie dish. Cut small pieces of pastry to fit around the pie funnel. Mark the pastry to lid size and cut out a hole to fit over the pie funnel. Use the remaining scraps to cut 2 cm strips to fit on the rim of the pie plate. Press the joins together. Brush the pie plate rim and strips with egg and water glaze, place on the pastry lid and press to seal. Use the back of a knife to push up the pastry edge at 2 cm intervals. Use any leftover scraps to make decorative cut-outs. Refrigerate for at least 30 minutes. Brush the pastry top with egg glaze. Preheat the oven to 210°C (190°C gas). Bake the pie for 30–40 minutes or until the pastry is golden brown and cooked through. Reduce the oven temperature to 180°C during the last 10 minutes of cooking and cover with foil to prevent the top browning too much. Serve immediately.

Add beer or cider to pan and stir constantly with wooden spoon for 3 minutes.

When the rabbit is cold, place the pie funnel in the centre of the dish.

～ Pork Pie ～

Preparation time:
**45 minutes +
refrigeration**
Total cooking time:
1 hour 45 minutes

Serves 6–8

3 cups plain flour
2 egg yolks
125 g lard, chopped
²⁄₃ cup water
600 g boneless pork
  cubes
4 rashers bacon,
  chopped
1 medium red onion,
  chopped
¹⁄₂ stick celery, chopped
1 tablespoon fresh
  thyme

1 cup fresh
  breadcrumbs
1 egg, lightly beaten
1 egg, lightly beaten,
  extra, for glazing

Aspic
¹⁄₂ cup apple juice or
  water
1 teaspoon chicken
  stock powder
2 teaspoons gelatine

1 ～Grease a deep round 17 cm diameter springform tin with melted butter or oil. Sift the flour into a large bowl. Make a well in the centre and add egg yolks. Cover the egg yolks with the flour and set aside. Place the lard and water in a small pan and stir over medium heat until the lard is melted. Bring to the boil and then quickly pour it over the flour and eggs. Using a wooden spoon, mix to a soft dough. Use your hands to bring together into a rough ball. Turn out onto a lightly floured surface and knead the dough for about 1 minute until smooth. Wrap in plastic wrap and refrigerate for 30 minutes.
2 ～Place the pork, in batches, in a food processor. Process the pork until roughly chopped but not minced. Transfer to a large bowl.

Add the bacon, onion, celery, thyme, breadcrumbs and egg. Mix until well combined and then cover and refrigerate.
3 ～Roll out two-thirds of the pastry, between 2 sheets of greaseproof paper, until big enough to line the base and side of the tin; trim the edges and brush with some of the extra egg. Spoon the filling firmly into the tin and smooth the surface. Roll the remaining pastry to a 20 cm diameter circle. Cut a 2 cm hole in the centre of the pastry. Fit over the filling, trim the pastry and press to seal edges together. Decorate with pastry scraps. Refrigerate for 30 minutes. Preheat oven to 210°C (190°C gas). Brush pie with the

extra egg. Bake for 45 minutes, reduce oven temperature to 180°C and continue to cook for 1 hour. Cover with foil if the pastry is browning too much. Allow to cool in tin.
4 ～**To make Aspic:** In a small pan, combine juice or water with stock powder, sprinkle over gelatine and stir over low heat until the gelatine has dissolved. Pour aspic a little at a time into the pie hole, allowing it to soak in between each addition. Cover the pie and refrigerate overnight. Remove from the tin. Serve this pie cold, cut into wedges.

Use your hands to bring the dough together to form a rough ball.

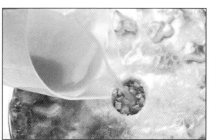
Pour a little aspic at a time into pie hole, allowing it to soak in between additions.

Sweet Pies

~ Freeform Blueberry Pie ~

Preparation time:
**20 minutes +
refrigeration**
Total cooking time:
30–35 minutes

Serves 4

1½ cups plain flour
125 g butter
½ cup icing sugar
  plus extra for
  dusting
¼ cup lemon juice
1 egg white, lightly
  beaten

500 g blueberries
¼ cup icing sugar
1 teaspoon finely grated
  lemon rind
½ teaspoon ground
  cinnamon

1.~Preheat the oven to 180°C. Place the flour, butter and icing sugar in a food processor. Process for 15 seconds or until fine and crumbly. Add almost all the juice, process briefly until mixture comes together, adding more juice if necessary.

2.~Turn the pastry out onto a sheet of baking paper and press together until smooth. Roll out to a circle about 30 cm in diameter and cover with plastic wrap. Refrigerate for 10 minutes. Place blueberries in a bowl; sprinkle sugar, rind and cinnamon over the top.

3.~Place pastry (still on baking paper) onto an oven tray. Brush centre of pastry lightly with egg white. Pile blueberry mixture onto pastry in a 20 cm diameter circle; fold edges of pastry over filling. Bake for 30–35 minutes. Dust top of the pie with icing sugar.

Process flour, butter and sugar in a food processor until mixture is fine and crumbly.

Press the pastry together until smooth, then roll into a circle about 30 cm in diameter.

Brush the centre of the rolled out pastry lightly with egg white.

Fold the edges of the pastry over blueberry mixture, leaving the filling showing.

~ Lemon Meringue Pie ~

Preparation time:
**30 minutes +
30 minutes standing
and refrigeration**
Total cooking time:
40 minutes

Serves 6

1¼ cups plain flour
2–3 tablespoons icing
  sugar
125 g butter, chopped
3 tablespoons iced
  water

Filling
¼ cup cornflour
⅓ cup water

1 cup lemon juice
2 teaspoons finely
  grated lemon rind
¾ cup caster sugar
6 egg yolks
30 g butter, chopped

Topping
6 egg whites
¾ cup caster sugar

---

1 ~ Sift the flour and icing sugar into a large bowl. Add the butter to the flour and rub them together with your fingertips for 2 minutes or until mixture is fine and crumbly. Add almost all the water and mix to a firm dough, adding more if necessary. Turn onto a lightly floured surface and press together until smooth. Roll between 2 sheets of plastic wrap until large enough to fit a 22 cm flan ring. Place ring on a flat oven tray, line with pastry and trim the edges. Refrigerate for 20 minutes. Preheat the oven to 180°C. Cut a sheet of greaseproof paper to cover the pastry. Spread a layer of dried beans or rice over the paper. Bake for 10 minutes. Remove from oven; discard beans or rice. Bake for another 10 minutes or until the pastry is lightly golden. Allow to cool. Turn the oven off.

2 ~ **To make Filling:** Place the cornflour and a little water in a small bowl; stir until smooth. Combine remaining water, juice, rind and sugar in small pan; stir without boiling until sugar dissolves. Add the cornflour mixture and stir until well combined. Stir over moderate heat until the mixture boils and thickens. Simmer, stirring, for another minute. Remove from heat and whisk in the egg yolks and butter. Transfer the mixture to a bowl, cover the surface with plastic wrap; allow to cool completely.

3 ~ **To make Topping:** Preheat the oven to 150°C. Using electric beaters, beat the egg whites in a small, dry bowl until soft peaks form. Add the caster sugar gradually, beating constantly until sugar has dissolved and the mixture is thick and glossy. Pour the cold filling into the cold pastry shell. Spread the meringue over the top, forming decorative peaks. Bake 20 minutes or until lightly browned. **Note** ~ The pie in the picture was baked in a pastry or flan ring, available from specialty shops. The ring is placed directly on a baking tray is easy to remove after baking, and gives the pastry a smooth finish. The pie can also be made in a 22 cm fluted flan tin or standard pie dish.

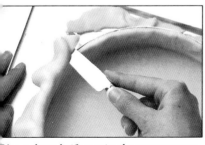

Use a sharp knife to trim the excess pastry from the top of the flan ring.

Covering the surface of the filling with plastic wrap stops a skin forming.

～ Pumpkin Pie ～

Preparation time:
**20 minutes +
20 minutes
refrigeration time**
Total cooking time:
1 hour

Serves 8

1¼ cups plain flour
100 g butter,
chopped
2 teaspoons caster
sugar
4 tablespoons water,
chilled
1 egg yolk, lightly
beaten, mixed with
1 tablespoon milk,
for glazing

Filling
2 eggs, lightly beaten
3/4 cup soft brown sugar
500 g pumpkin,
cooked, mashed and
cooled
1/3 cup cream
1 tablespoon sweet
sherry
1 teaspoon ground
cinnamon
1/2 teaspoon ground
nutmeg
1/2 teaspoon ground
ginger

1.～Sift the flour into a large bowl and add chopped butter. Using your fingertips, rub the butter into the flour for 2 minutes or until the mixture is fine and crumbly. Stir in the caster sugar. Add almost all the water and mix to a firm dough, adding more if necessary. Turn onto a lightly floured surface, press together for 1 minute or until smooth.

2.～Roll out the pastry, on a sheet of baking paper, until it is large enough to cover the base and side of 23 cm diameter pie dish. Line the dish with pastry, trim away excess and crimp the edges. Roll out the pastry trimmings to 2 mm thickness. Using a sharp knife, cut out leaf shapes of different sizes. Score vein markings onto the leaves. Refrigerate the pastry-lined dish and the leaf shapes for about 20 minutes.

3.～Preheat the oven to 180°C. Cut a sheet of greaseproof paper to cover the pastry-lined dish. Spread a layer of dried beans or rice over the paper. Bake for 10 minutes, remove from the oven and discard the paper and beans. Return pastry to the oven for 10 minutes or until lightly golden. Meanwhile, place the leaves on an oven tray lined with baking paper, brush with egg glaze and bake for 10–15 minutes, until golden; set aside to cool.

4.～**To make Filling:** Whisk the eggs and sugar in a large bowl.

Add the cooled pumpkin, cream, sweet sherry and spices, and stir to combine thoroughly. Pour the mixture into the pastry shell, smooth the surface with the back of a spoon, and then bake for 40 minutes or until set. If the pastry edges begin to brown too much during cooking, cover the edges with foil. Allow the pie to cool to room temperature and then place the leaves on top of the filling.
Pumpkin pie may be served with cream or ice cream, if desired.

On a lightly floured surface, press the dough together gently until it is smooth.

Add cooled pumpkin, cream, sherry and spices to egg and stir until well combined.

~Key Lime Pie ~

Preparation time:
25 minutes
Total cooking time:
**25 minutes +
2 hours refrigeration**

Serves 8

125 g sweet wheatmeal biscuits	½ cup lime juice
80 g butter, melted	2 teaspoons finely grated lime rind
4 egg yolks	1 cup cream, whipped
400 g can condensed milk	lime rind, for garnish

1~Place the biscuits in a food processor and process for 30 seconds or until finely crushed.
2~Transfer to a bowl, add the butter and mix until the crumbs are well moistened. Press into a 23 cm diameter pie dish;

refrigerate until firm. Preheat oven to 180°C.
3~Using electric beaters, beat the yolks, condensed milk, lime juice and rind in a large bowl for 1 minute or until combined. Pour into crust and smooth the surface. Bake for 20–25 minutes until set.

4~Allow pie to cool; refrigerate for 2 hours or until well chilled. Decorate with whipped cream and lime rind.
Note~A small tool called a zester, available from kitchenware shops or department stores, is handy for making strips of lime rind.

Process the wheatmeal biscuits in a food processor until finely crushed.

Press the crumb mixture on side and base of a 23 cm diameter pie dish.

Beat the egg yolks, condensed milk, lime juice and rind until well combined.

Using a zester, make strips of lime rind to decorate the pie.

~ Cherry Pie ~

Preparation time:
**25 minutes +
refrigeration**
Total cooking time:
40 minutes

Serves 6–8

2 x 700 g jars pitted morello cherries, drained	100 g butter, chopped
1¼ cups plain flour	3 tablespoons iced water
¼ cup icing sugar	1 egg, lightly beaten
⅓ cup ground almonds	caster sugar, for decoration

1 ~ Spread the cherries into a 23 cm diameter pie dish. Sift the flour and icing sugar into a mixing bowl and then stir in the ground almonds. Add the butter and rub in with your fingertips until the mixture is fine and crumbly. Add almost all the water and cut into the flour mixture with a knife until mixture forms a dough, adding remaining water if necessary.
2 ~ Turn the dough out onto a lightly floured surface and press together until smooth.

Roll out on a sheet of baking paper a circle of about 26 cm diameter. Cover with plastic wrap and refrigerate for about 15 minutes.
3 ~ Preheat the oven to 200°C. Cover the pie dish with the pastry and trim the overhanging edges. Roll out the remaining scraps of pastry and use a small sharp knife to cut out decorations. Brush the pastry top all over with beaten egg and arrange the decorations on top. Brush these with beaten egg as well, and then sprinkle lightly with caster sugar. Place the pie

dish on a baking tray (the cherry juice may overflow from the side a little) and cook for 35–40 minutes or until golden brown. Serve warm or at room temperature, with cream or ice cream, if you like.

Note ~ Refrigerating pastry for about 15 minutes after rolling it out allows it to 'rest' and prevents it from shrinking too much during cooking.

Add the butter to the flour, using your fingertips to rub it in until fine and crumbly.

Brush the beaten egg all over the top of the pastry, using a pastry brush.

~ Apple Pie ~

Preparation time:
**35 minutes +
refrigeration**
Total cooking time:
1 hour

Serves 6

2 cups plain flour
1/4 cup icing sugar
185 g cold butter, cubed
2 egg yolks
2–3 tablespoons cold
water
milk, for glazing

Apple Filling
4–5 medium green
cooking apples, peeled,
cored and sliced
3/4 cup caster sugar plus
extra for decoration
2 tablespoons water
1/2 teaspoon ground
cinnamon
6 whole cloves
1 tablespoon marmalade
30 g butter

1 ~Brush a 23 cm diameter pie dish with melted butter or oil. Place the flour, icing sugar and butter in a food processor. Process for 30 seconds or until the mixture is fine and crumbly. Add the egg yolks and the water and process for 20 seconds or until the mixture just comes together. Add more water if necessary to form dough.

2 ~Turn onto a lightly floured surface and knead briefly to form a smooth dough. Divide the pastry into 2 portions, one slightly larger than the other. Roll the larger portion between 2 sheets of baking paper to fit into the pie dish and trim the edges. Roll the remaining pastry on a sheet of baking paper to fit the top of the dish. Cover both pastries and refrigerate.

3 ~**To make Apple Filling:** Combine the apples, sugar, water, cinnamon and cloves in a large pan. Cover and cook over low heat, stirring occasionally, for 20 minutes or until just softened. Remove pan from heat and pour off any excess juice. Remove cloves from pan. Add marmalade and butter to pan, mix gently and set aside to cool.

4 ~Preheat the oven to 210°C (190°C gas). Pile the apples evenly into the pastry-lined pie dish. Brush the pie rim with milk or water. Place the pastry lid over the apples and press the edges to seal. Trim the pastry and seal the edges with a fork. Use a pastry or biscuit cutter to cut shapes from the leftover

pastry and place the shapes on top of the pie. Slash 2 or 3 small holes in the pastry to allow steam to escape. Brush the surface of pie with milk and sprinkle with extra caster sugar. Bake for 10 minutes. Reduce the oven temperature to 180°C and bake for another 30 minutes or until pastry is golden brown. Serve with cream or ice cream, if you like.

Note ~Apple pie is delicious cold or at room temperature, served at a picnic. Apple pie also freezes well. You can make two at once and freeze one. Wrap well, seal and label before freezing.

∽ Bramble Pie ∽

Preparation time:
**30 minutes +
refrigeration**
Total cooking time:
40 minutes

Serves 4–6

1 cup self-raising flour
1 cup plain flour
125 g cold butter, cubed
2 tablespoons caster sugar
1 egg, lightly beaten
3–4 tablespoons milk
1 egg yolk, extra, mixed with 1 teaspoon water, for glazing
icing sugar, for dusting

Bramble Filling
2 tablespoons cornflour
2–4 tablespoons caster sugar, to taste
1 teaspoon grated orange rind
1 tablespoon orange juice
600 g fresh brambles (see Note)

1 ∽ Place the flours, butter and caster sugar in a food processor. Process for 30 seconds or until the mixture is fine and crumbly. Add the egg and almost all the milk; process for another 15 seconds or until the mixture comes together, adding more milk if necessary. Turn onto a lightly floured surface and knead briefly to form a smooth dough. Divide the dough into 2 portions. Roll each portion out on a sheet of baking paper, making sure one is the right size to fit the top of a 3-cup capacity pie dish. Cover with plastic wrap and refrigerate for 30 minutes.

2 ∽ **To make Bramble Filling:** Place the cornflour, caster sugar, orange rind and juice in a medium pan; mix well to combine. Add half the brambles to the pan. Stir over low heat for 5 minutes or until the mixture boils and thickens. Remove the pan from the heat and set aside to allow the mixture to cool. Add the remaining brambles to the pan. Pour the mixture into the pie dish and smooth the surface using the back of a spoon.

3 ∽ Preheat the oven to 180°C. Place the pie top over the fruit and trim the edges. Using heart-shaped pastry cutters of various sizes, cut out enough hearts to cover the pie top and then place them on top of the pie in a random fashion.

4 ∽ Brush the surface of the pie with the egg glaze. Bake for 35 minutes or until the pastry is crisp and golden brown. Sprinkle the top with icing sugar before serving.

Note ∽ Brambles include any creeping stem berries, such as boysenberries, blackberries, loganberries and youngberries. Use just one variety or a combination if you prefer. This pie is perfect to make when there is a glut of these berries. However, if you want to make the pie when the berries are out of season, look for the frozen variety in supermarkets or specialist stores. You can use canned berries if you drain them well first. This pie may be served warm or cold.

When the mixture has thickened, add the remaining brambles to the pan and stir.

Place heart-shaped cut-outs on the pie in a random fashion, to decorate.

~ Mulberry and Apple Pie ~

Preparation time:
**30 minutes +
refrigeration**
Total cooking time:
45 minutes

Serves 4–6

2 cups plain flour	caster sugar, for
1/4 cup caster sugar	decoration
1 teaspoon grated	
orange rind	*Filling*
185 g cold butter, cubed	410 g can pie apples
2 egg yolks	1/4 cup caster sugar
2–3 tablespoons cold	1 tablespoon cornflour
water	500 g fresh mulberries,
egg yolk and water,	stems removed
extra	
1 egg white, for glazing	

1 ∼ Place the flour, sugar, rind and butter in a food processor. Process for 30 seconds or until the mixture is fine and crumbly. Add the egg yolks and 2 tablespoons of the water; process for 20 seconds or until the mixture just comes together. Add more water if necessary. Turn onto a lightly floured surface and knead briefly to form a smooth dough. Remove one quarter of the dough. Roll the larger portion out on a sheet of baking paper to a 25 cm diameter circle. Roll the smaller portion into a rectangle. Refrigerate until required.

2 ∼ **To make Filling:** Place the apples, sugar and cornflour in a small pan and stir over low heat for 2–3 minutes until the mixture is slightly thickened.

Set aside to cool. Add the mulberries to the apples and gently fold through. Add more sugar to taste, if necessary. Spoon into a 23 cm diameter pie dish and smooth the surface. Brush the outer rim of the pie dish with combined egg yolk and water.

3 ∼ Preheat the oven to 210°C (190°C gas). Place the pastry circle over the pie and trim the edges. Using a pastry wheel, cut strips 1 cm wide from the remaining pastry and place them in a pattern on top of the pie. Cut a small circle to place in the centre of the pattern.

4 ∼ Brush the surface of the pie with egg white and sprinkle generously with caster sugar. Bake for 10 minutes, reduce the oven temperature

to 180°C and bake the pie for another 30 minutes or until the pastry is golden. Serve immediately with crème fraîche or ice cream, if you like.

Note: ∼ You can use fresh raspberries if mulberries are not in season. This pie can be frozen before or after baking. If baking before freezing, cook it for about 10 minutes less than normal to prevent excessive browning. If unbaked, cook from frozen, except bake at 180°C for an extra 10–20 minutes. If browning too much, cover with foil. Freeze for 6 months if unbaked or 4 months if baked.

Using a pastry wheel, cut strips of pastry cm wide to place in a pattern on the pie.

After brushing the pie top with egg white, sprinkle it generously with caster sugar.

～ Apricot Almond Pie ～

Preparation time:
**40 minutes +
refrigeration**
Total cooking time:
1 hour

Serves 6–8

185 g butter, at room
  temperature
1/3 cup caster sugar
2 eggs
1 cup plain flour
1 1/4 cups self-raising
  flour
1/4 cup custard powder
1/2 cup flaked almonds,
  for topping
icing sugar, for dusting

Apricot Filling
2 x 425 g cans apricot
  pie filling
1/4 cup soft brown sugar
1 teaspoon grated
  lemon rind
1/2 cup ground almonds
1 teaspoon amaretto
  (almond) liqueur,
  optional

1. Place the butter and sugar in a bowl and beat, using electric beaters, until light and creamy. Add an egg. Separate the other egg and add the egg yolk to the bowl, reserving the white for glazing. Beat the mixture until combined. Mix in combined sifted flours and custard powder with a knife to form a soft dough. Turn out onto a lightly floured surface and knead lightly until the mixture forms a smooth ball. Refrigerate, covered in plastic wrap, for 30 minutes.

2. **To make Apricot Filling:** In a medium bowl, place the apricots, sugar, lemon rind, almonds and liqueur. Stir until well combined.

3. Brush a deep, fluted 25 cm flan tin with melted butter or oil. Roll out two-thirds of the pastry between 2 sheets of baking paper. Line the prepared tin with pastry and trim the edges. Push the pastry down into the tin so it comes about 2 cm from the top. Pile the Apricot Filling into the tin and level the apricots. Roll out the remaining pastry to a 21 cm diameter circle and fit on top of the pie, pressing gently to seal. Make 3–4 slits in the top of pie to allow steam to escape. Refrigerate for 30 minutes.

4. Preheat the oven to 210°C (190°C gas). Bake the pie for 10 minutes. Reduce the oven temperature to 180°C and continue to cook for another 45–50 minutes. After 25 minutes of baking, remove the pie from the oven and quickly brush the surface with lightly beaten egg white. Scatter almonds over the top and return the pie to the oven until the pastry is cooked and golden brown. If the almonds start to brown too much, cover the pie with foil. Dust the top lightly with icing sugar before serving. Serve hot with cream or custard.

Note This pastry is very soft and fragile. When any splits or holes occur while you are handling it, simply patch with extra pastry or press the splits back together. Keep the pastry cold to make it easier to work with and use only your fingertips.

～ Fruit Mince Pies ～

Preparation time:
30 minutes
Total cooking time:
25 minutes

Makes 24

2 cups plain flour	1 tablespoon chopped
2/3 cup icing sugar	almonds
150 g butter	1 small apple, grated
2–3 tablespoons iced	1 teaspoon lemon juice
water	1/2 teaspoon finely
icing sugar, for dusting	grated orange rind
	1/2 teaspoon finely
Fruit Mince	grated lemon rind
1/3 cup raisins, chopped	1/2 teaspoon mixed spice
1/3 cup brown sugar	pinch nutmeg
1/4 cup sultanas	25 g melted butter
1/4 cup mixed peel	1 tablespoon brandy
1 tablespoon currants	

1～Preheat the oven to 180°C. Brush two 12-cup shallow patty tins lightly with melted butter.

2～Place flour, sugar and butter in a food processor. Process until the mixture is fine and crumbly. Add almost all the water and process until the mixture comes together. Turn onto a lightly floured surface, press together until smooth. Roll out two-thirds of the pastry and use a biscuit cutter to cut out 24 circles. Fit the circles into prepared tins.

3～Divide Fruit Mince between pastry cases. Roll out the remaining pastry, cut out 12 circles with the same cutter. Using a smaller, fluted cutter, cut a circle from the centre of each. Place large circles on tops of pies, press edges to seal. Place smaller circles on remainder. Bake for 25 minutes or until golden. Leave in the tins for 5 minutes and then carefully lift out with a knife and allow to cool on wire racks. Dust tops lightly with icing sugar.

4～**To make Fruit Mince:** Combine all the ingredients in a bowl. Spoon into a sterilised jar. You can use the fruit mince straight away but the flavours develop if kept for a while. You can keep it, in a cool dark place, for up to 3 months. This recipe makes about 1 1/4 cups. **Note**～Ready-made fruit mince can be used instead but the flavour will be less intense.

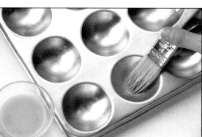

Brush the shallow patty tins lightly with melted butter.

Process the flour, sugar and butter in a food processor until fine and crumbly.

From the centre of each of the 12 tops, use a smaller fluted cutter to cut 12 more tops.

Use a wooden spoon to combine all the fruit mince ingredients in a bowl.

~Apple Crumble Pie~

Preparation time:
**30 minutes +
refrigeration**
Total cooking time:
30 minutes

Serves 4–6

8 pitted prunes
1/4 cup dried apricots
1/4 cup muscatels or
    raisins
3/4 cup apple juice
410 g can pie apples
1 tablespoon caster
    sugar
1 teaspoon grated
    orange rind

1 cup plain flour
1 tablespoon caster
    sugar
90 g cold butter, cubed
2–3 tablespoons cold
    water
1 tablespoon soft brown
    sugar
50 g ground hazelnuts

1 Place the prunes, apricots and muscatels in a bowl and cover with apple juice. Leave to soak for a minimum of 1 hour. Drain well and combine with the pie apples, sugar and orange rind. Pour into a 20 cm diameter pie plate, smooth surface, cover and set aside.

2 Place the flour, sugar and butter in a food processor. Process for 30 seconds or until the mixture is fine and crumbly. Add 2 tablespoons of the water and process for 20 seconds or until the mixture just comes together. Add more water if necessary to form the dough.

3 Turn onto a lightly floured surface and knead briefly to form a smooth dough. Cover with plastic wrap and refrigerate for a minimum of 1 hour. Grate three-quarters of the dough into a large bowl. Using your hands, gently mix through the brown sugar and hazelnuts. Spread the mixture evenly over the fruit in the pie dish.

4 Roll the remaining pastry into two thin strands, 60 cm long, and twist together to form a rope. Place around the edge of the pastry to form a pastry rim. Refrigerate for 30 minutes. Preheat the oven to 210°C (190°C gas). Bake for 10 minutes, reduce the heat to 180°C and bake for another 20 minutes or until the pastry is cooked through and browned. Serve the pie hot or warm, with cream or ice cream, if desired.

After refrigerating the dough for at least an hour, grate three-quarters of it into a bowl.

To make a rope for the rim of the pie, twist two thin, long strands of pastry together.

～ Rhubarb Lattice Pie ～

Preparation time:
**35 minutes +
refrigeration**
Total cooking time:
1 hour

Serves 4–6

1¼ cups plain flour
¼ teaspoon baking
  powder
1 tablespoon caster
  sugar
90 g cold butter, cubed
3–4 tablespoons cold
  water
milk, for glazing
demerara sugar, for
  decoration

Rhubarb Filling
1 bunch rhubarb,
  trimmed and washed
  (about 500 g)
½ cup caster sugar
5 cm piece orange rind
1 tablespoon orange
  juice
410 g can pie apples

1 ～Preheat the oven to 180°C. Place the flour, baking powder, sugar and butter in a food processor. Process for 30 seconds or until the mixture is fine and crumbly. Add almost all the water and process for 20 seconds or until the mixture just comes together. Add more water if necessary. Turn onto a lightly floured surface and knead briefly to form a smooth dough. Place the dough between 2 sheets of baking paper and roll out a circle of pastry about 28 cm in diameter. Refrigerate the pastry for 20 minutes.

2 ～**To make Rhubarb Filling:** Cut the rhubarb into 3 cm lengths. Combine it in a large casserole dish with the sugar, orange rind and juice. Cover the dish with a lid or foil and bake for 30 minutes or until the rhubarb is just tender. Remove the casserole dish from the oven, drain away any excess juice, remove and discard the rind. Set the rhubarb aside to cool. Add the apple and stir. Add more sugar, to taste, if necessary. Pour the mixture into a 20 cm diameter pie plate and smooth the surface. Increase the oven temperature to 210°C (190°C gas).

3 ～ Remove the pastry from the refrigerator and cut it into strips. Lay half of the strips on a sheet of baking paper, leaving a 1 cm gap between each strip. Interweave the remaining strips to form a lattice pattern. Cover with plastic and refrigerate, keeping it flat, until firm.

4 ～Place the pastry on top of the pie and bake the pie for 10 minutes. Remove the pie from the oven and quickly and lightly brush the pastry with milk and then sprinkle with demerara sugar. Reduce the oven temperature to 180°C and return the pie to the oven. Cook for 20 minutes or until the pastry is golden and the filling is bubbling. Serve with cream or ice cream, if desired.

Note ～When buying rhubarb it should be firm, crisp and not too large. Remove and discard any leaves as they are poisonous.

~ Deep Dish Apple Pie ~

Preparation time:
**1 hour +
refrigeration**
Total cooking time:
50 minutes

Serves 6–8

1 cup self-raising flour
1 cup plain flour
125 g chilled butter,
  chopped
2 tablespoons caster
  sugar
1 egg
1–2 tablespoons milk
1 egg, extra, lightly
  beaten, for glazing

Filling
8 large green apples,
  peeled, cored and
  cut into 12 wedges
2 thick strips lemon
  rind
6 whole cloves
1 cinnamon stick
2 cups water
1/2 cup sugar

1 ～Brush a deep, 20 cm diameter springform tin with melted butter or oil. Line the base with paper and grease the paper, dust lightly with flour and shake off excess.

2 ～Place the flours, butter and sugar in a food processor. Process for 15 seconds or until the mixture is fine and crumbly. Add the egg and almost all the milk and process for another 15 seconds or until the mixture comes together, adding more liquid if necessary. Turn onto a lightly floured surface, knead for 2 minutes or until smooth. Roll two-thirds of the pastry between 2 sheets of plastic wrap until large enough to cover base and side of tin. Roll out remaining pastry on a sheet of baking paper large enough to fit top of tin. Refrigerate pastry for 20 minutes.

3 ～**To make Filling:** Combine apples, rind, cloves, cinnamon, water and sugar in a large pan. Cover and simmer for 10 minutes or until tender. Remove from heat, drain well. Set aside until cold. Discard rind, cloves and cinnamon.

4 ～Preheat the oven to 180°C. Carefully spoon apples into the pie shell. Cover with the pie top. Brush pastry edges with a little of the extra beaten egg to seal. Prick top of the pie with a fork. Trim edges with a sharp knife, crimp edges to seal. Brush top with beaten egg. Bake for 50 minutes or until pastry is cooked through. Leave pie in tin for 10 minutes before removing.

Dust the lined tin lightly with flour and shake off any excess.

Cover the base and side of tin with the prepared pastry.

...ombine apples, cloves, rind, cinnamon ...ick, water and sugar in a large pan.

Prick the top of the pie a few times with a fork and then trim and crimp the edges.

~ Custards and Creams ~

Some sweet pies are especially delicious when served with a small dollop of flavoured custard or cream such as one chosen from the simple selection shown here.

Liqueur Custard

Using a wire whisk, beat 3 egg yolks and 2 tablespoons of sugar in a bowl for about 3 minutes, until the mixture is very light and creamy. Heat $1^1/2$ cups of milk in a small pan until just boiling, then pour slowly onto the egg mixture, whisking constantly. Return to the pan and stir with a wooden spoon over very low heat for about 5 minutes, until custard thickens. Do not allow the mixture to boil or it will curdle. Remove from the heat and stir in 1–2 tablespoons of your favourite liqueur or spirit.
Serves 6–8.

Mascarpone Brandy Cream

Place 250 g of mascarpone, $1/2$ cup of cream and 1 tablespoon of caster sugar in a bowl. Stir until thoroughly combined. Place 2 egg whites in a bowl and beat until mixture forms firm peaks. Fold mixture through the mascarpone mixture with a metal spoon. Add brandy to taste (about 1–2 tablespoons) and stir to combine. Refrigerate for at least 1 hour before serving.
Serves 8.

Sabayon

Place 4 egg yolks and 1/4 cup of caster sugar into a large heatproof bowl. Using electric beaters, beat for 1 minute until the mixture is light and creamy. Stand the bowl over a pan of barely simmering water, add 1/2 cup of sweet white wine and continue beating for 5 minutes, until the mixture is thick, light and foamy. Serve immediately, as the Sabayon will separate if left standing. Serves 8.

Yoghurt Cream

Whisk 1 cup of plain yoghurt, 1/2 cup of sour cream, 1 teaspoon of vanilla essence and 2 teaspoons of soft brown sugar together in a glass or ceramic bowl. Refrigerate for at least 8 hours before serving—the cream will thicken slightly. Serves 6.

Orange Ricotta Cream

Place 250 g of ricotta cheese, 1/2 cup of cream, 1 teaspoon of finely grated orange rind and 2 tablespoons of caster sugar in a bowl. Beat with electric beaters for a minute until combined and smooth. Add 2 tablespoons of Grand Marnier, if you like, and beat until just mixed through. Refrigerate for 1 hour before serving. Serves 6–8.

From left to right: Liqueur Custard, Mascarpone Brandy Cream, Yoghurt Cream, Sabayon, Orange Ricotta Cream

～ Index ～

Front cover photograph (from top left): Key Lime Pie (page 42), Chicken Pot Pies, (page 20), Chicken and Leek Pie, (page 28).